THE BEST

DOCTOR

JOKES EVER

THE BEST
DOCTOR
JOKES EVER

MetroBooks

There are several different kinds of doctors, and it is told that they can be differentiated by the following method:

General Practitioners know nothing and do little.

Surgeons know little and do everything.

Internists know everything and do nothing.

Pathologists know everything and can do everything, but it's usually too late.

PETE WAS SITTING AT HOME ONE evening when the doorbell rang. He opened the door to see a 6-foot-tall cockroach standing on his doorstep. The cockroach punched Pete between the eyes and scampered off.

The next evening, Pete was sitting at home when the doorbell rang. When he answered the door, the cockroach was there yet again. This time, he hit Pete, kicked him in the stomach, and karate chopped him on the back before running away.

The third evening, Pete was again sitting at home when he heard the doorbell. He answered the door, and, for the third time, the cockroach was there. It leapt at him and managed to stab him several times before running off. The gravely injured Pete was barely able to crawl to the telephone and summon an ambulance. He was rushed to intensive care, where they saved his life.

The next morning, the doctor was doing his rounds. He stopped by Pete's hospital room and asked him what happened. Pete explained about the 6-foot-tall cockroach's attacks, culminating in the near-fatal stabbing.

The doctor looked thoughtful for a moment and said, "Yes, there's a nasty bug going around."

Kerri, a veterinarian, was feeling ill and went to see Dr. West. He began to ask all the usual questions—her symptoms, duration, and the like—when Kerri suddenly cut him off.

"Hey, look, I'm a vet," she declared. "I don't need to ask *my* patients these kinds of questions—I can tell what's wrong just by looking at them. Why can't you?"

The doctor just nodded in response, looked Kerri up and down, and wrote out a prescription. He handed it to her and said, "There you are. Now of course, if *that* doesn't work, we'll have to have you put down."

A WELL-KNOWN, RICH BUSINESSMAN'S wife broke her hip. The businessman got the best orthopedic surgeon in town to do the operation, which consisted of lining up the broken hip and putting in a screw to secure it.

The operation went smoothly, and the doctor sent the businessman a bill for $5,000 for his services. The businessman, outraged at the high price, sent the doctor a letter demanding an itemized list of the costs. The doctor responded to the letter with the following:

1 Screw: $1
Knowing how to put it in: $4,999
Total: $5,000
The businessman never argued.

A doctor and his wife were sunbathing on a beach when a beautiful young blonde in a tight-fitting bikini strolled past. The blonde looked at the doctor, smiled seductively, and murmured in a very sexy voice, "Hi there, handsome. How ya doin'?" She then wiggled her backside and walked off.

"Who was that?" demanded the doctor's wife.

"Er—just a woman I met professionally," stammered the doctor.

"Oh yeah?" his wife snarled. "In whose profession? Yours or hers?"

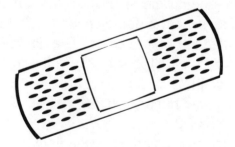

BARRY WENT TO DR. THOMAS AND SAID, "Doc, I would like to live for a long time. Do you have any advice?"

"Well, now. I commend you for your wise decision," Dr. Thomas replied heartily. "Let's see here. Do you smoke?"

"Oh, maybe a half a pack a day."

"Starting now, no more smoking." Barry agreed.

Dr. Thomas then asked, "Do you drink?"

"Oh, well now, Doc, not much—just a bit of wine with some meals and a beer or two once in a while."

"Starting now, you drink only water. No exceptions." Barry was a bit upset by now, but he nonetheless agreed.

"Do you have sex?" the doctor asked.

"Yeah, once a week or so—but only with my wife!" he added hurriedly.

"As soon as you get out of here you are going to buy twin beds. No more sex for you. None."

Barry was appalled. "Doc, this is nuts. I guess I can understand the diet and the drinking and all that, but jeez—no more sex?

Are you sure I'm going to live longer this way?"

"I have no idea, but however long you live, I assure you it is going to seem like an eternity!"

It was a stifling hot day and a man fainted in the middle of a busy intersection. Traffic quickly piled up in all directions and a woman rushed over to help him. As she knelt down to loosen his collar, a man emerged from the crowd, pushed her aside and said, "It's all right, honey. I've had a course in first aid."

The woman stood up and watched as he took the ill man's pulse and prepared to administer artificial respiration. At this point she tapped him on the shoulder and said, "When you get to the part about calling the doctor, I'm already here."

THE DOCTOR TOOK DAN INTO THE ROOM and said, "Dan, I have some good news and some bad news."

"Oh, no. Give me the good news, I guess," Dan replied.

"They're going to name a disease after you."

A college physics professor was explaining a particularly complicated concept to his class when a pre-med student interrupted him.

"Why do we have to learn this stuff?" the frustrated student blurted out.

"To save lives," the professor responded before continuing the lecture.

A few minutes later the student spoke up again. "So how does physics save lives?"

The professor stared at the student without saying a word. "Physics saves lives," he finally continued, "because it keeps the idiots out of medical school."

A MOTHER, MRS. JONES, TOOK HER sixteen-year-old daughter to the doctor.

"Doctor, it's my daughter, Amy," Mrs. Jones said. "She keeps getting these cravings. She's sick most mornings, but yet she keeps putting on weight."

The doctor gave Amy a thorough examination, then turned to the mother. "Well, I don't know how to tell you this, but your Amy is pregnant—about four months would be my guess."

Mrs. Jones was astonished. "Pregnant! She can't be—Amy has never even been alone with a man!" She turned to her daughter. "Isn't that right, dear?"

"That's right, Mother!" Amy insisted. "I've never even kissed a man!"

The doctor walked to the window and stared through the glass. Three minutes later, he still had not said a word. Finally Mrs. Jones asked, "Is there something wrong out there, doctor?"

"No, not really," the doctor replied. "It's just that the last time anything like this happened, a star appeared in the east and three wise men came over the hill. I'll be darned if I'm going to miss it this time!"

Dr. Benson, a surgical resident, was called out of a sound sleep to the emergency room. Unshaven and with tousled hair, he showed up with an equally unpresentable medical student. In the ER, they encountered the on-call medical resident and his student, both neatly attired in clean white lab coats.

The medical resident commented to his student, "You can always tell the surgeons by their absolute disregard for appearance."

Two evenings later, Benson was at a banquet when he was called to the ER to suture a minor laceration. He was stitching away, still wearing a tuxedo, when he encountered the same medical resident.

He looked at Benson, then said to his student, "Sure is sensitive to criticism, isn't he?"

THE WHOLE NEIGHBORHOOD SHOOK from the explosion. As shopkeepers ran outside to see what happened, they spotted the pharmacist staggering out of his smoldering building. His white coat was scorched black. He went up to a woman standing nearby.

"Lady," he said. "Would you please ask your doctor to write that prescription again. And this time, tell him to *print* it!"

M rs. Jones went to see her obstetrician. "Dr. Smith, I'm pregnant again. I need a hearing aid."

"Mrs. Jones," Dr. Smith said, "I thought we decided last time that twelve children were more than you could handle. You don't need a hearing aid—what you need is a more powerful contraceptive."

Mrs. Jones insisted. "But Dr. Smith, I don't need a contraceptive. I need a hearing aid."

"I don't understand," said Dr. Smith.

"Well, you see, Doctor," replied Mrs. Jones, "I'm kind of hard of hearing. At night, when the mister and I turn off the lights and go to bed, he asks me, 'Do you want to go to sleep or what?' And I always say, 'What?'"

THE PATIENT'S FAMILY GATHERED AT the hospital to hear what the specialists had to say about their beloved.

"Things don't look good," the doctor began. "The only chance he has is with a brain transplant. Now, you should know that this is an experimental procedure. It might work; it might not. Either way, brains are very expensive and you would have to cover the cost on your own."

"Well, how much does the brain cost?" piped up one relative.

"A male brain is $500,000. A female brain, $200,000."

Some of the younger male relatives tried to look shocked, but the rest of the men nodded, thinking they understood. A few actually smirked. But the patient's daughter was unsatisfied. "Why the large difference in price between male brains and female brains?" she asked.

"A standard pricing practice," said the head of the team. "Women's brains have to be marked down because they've actually been used."

The doctors were told to contribute to the construction of a new wing at a hospital. The allergists voted to scratch it; the dermatologists preferred no rash moves; the gastroenterologists had a gut feeling about it; the microsurgeons were thinking along the same vein; the neurologists thought the administration "had a lot of nerve"; the obstetricians stated they were laboring under a misconception; the opthomologists considered the idea short-sighted; the orthopedists issued a joint resolution; the pathologists yelled, "Over my dead body!"; the pediatricians said, "Grow up"; the psychiatrists thought it was madness; and finally, the surgeons decided to wash their hands of the whole thing.

The radiologists could see right through it; the internists thought it was a hard pill to swallow; the plastic surgeons said, "This puts a whole new face on the matter"; the podiatrists thought it was a big step forward; the urologists thought the scheme wouldn't hold water; the anesthesiologists thought the whole idea was a gas; the cardiologists didn't have the heart to say no; and the otologists were deaf to the idea.

Needless to say, the idea of contributing to a new wing didn't fly!

PSYCHIATRIST TO HIS NURSE: "JUST say we're very busy. Don't keep saying 'It's a madhouse.'"

O n a busy Med/Surg floor, Dr. Thompson
stopped Nurse Berry to brief her on a
patient's condition. "This patient is a
fellow physician and my favorite golf partner.
His injury is serious, and I fear he will not be
able to play golf again, unless you follow my
orders to a tee."

Dr. Thompson then began to bark instructions: "You must give an injection in a different location every twenty minutes, followed by
a second injection exactly five minutes after
the first. He must take two pills at exactly
every hour followed by one pill every fifteen
minutes for eight hours. Soak his arm in warm
water for fifteen minutes then place ice for
ten minutes and repeat for the rest of the
day. Give range of motion every thirty
minutes. He requires a back rub and foot rub
every hour. Feed him something tasty every
hour. Be cheerful and do whatever he asks at
all times, and be sure to chart his condition
and vital signs every twenty minutes. You must
do these things exactly as I ordered or his
injury will not heal properly, and he will never
be able to golf again."

Nurse Berry left the doctor and entered the patient's room. The anxious family and the equally anxious patient greeted her. All asked the nurse what the doctor had said about the condition of the patient.

"The doctor said that you will live." Nurse Berry quickly reviewed the orders. Then she added, "But you will have to learn a new sport."

MARGIE RECEIVED A BILL FROM THE hospital for her recent surgery, and was astonished to see a $900 fee for the anesthesiologist. She called his office to demand an explanation.

"Is this some kind of mistake?" Margie asked when she got the doctor on the phone.

"No, not at all," the doctor said calmly.

"Well," said Margie, "that's awfully costly for knocking someone out."

"No," replied the doctor. "I knock you out for free. The 900 bucks is for bringing you back around."

A seven-year-old girl came home from school and told her mother, "A boy in my class asked me to play doctor."

"Oh, dear," the mother said nervously. "What happened, honey?"

"Nothing. He made me wait forty-five minutes and then double-billed the insurance company."

SEEMS AN ELDERLY GENTLEMAN HAD serious hearing problems for a number of years. He finally decided to see Dr. Ellenberg, who had him fitted for a set of hearing aids.

The elderly gentleman went back in a month to the doctor. Dr. Ellenberg checked his hearing, and after the exam was complete said, "Your hearing is perfect. Your family must be so pleased that you can hear again."

"Oh, I haven't told my family yet," the gentleman replied. "I just sit around and listen to conversations. I changed my will three times last month!"

ONE PLASTIC SURGEON TO ANOTHER:
"My daughter gets her good looks from me."

Dr. Weathers, a psychologist, was walking along a Hawaiian beach when she kicked a bottle poking up through the sand. She opened it and was astonished to see a cloud of smoke. Out came a genie smiling upon her.

"For your kindness," the genie said, "I will grant you one wish!"

The psychologist paused, laughed, and then replied, "I have always wanted a road from Hawaii to California."

The genie grimaced, thought for a few minutes, and said, "Listen, I'm sorry, but I can't do that. Think of all the pilings needed to hold up the highway and how long they'd have to be to reach the bottom of the ocean. Think of all the pavement that would be needed. I hate to say it, but that's just too much to ask."

"Okay," replied the psychologist, not wanting to be unreasonable. "I'm a psychologist. Make me understand my patients. What makes them laugh and cry? Why are they temperamental, and what makes it so difficult to get along with them? What do they *really* want? Basically, teach me to understand what makes them tick!"

The genie paused, and then sighed. "Did you want two lanes or four?"

A t a major medical convention, a noted internist arose to announce that he had discovered a new miracle antibiotic.

"What does it cure?" asked a member of the audience.

"Nothing we don't already have a drug for," the internist replied.

"Well, what's so miraculous about it?" another doctor called out.

The internist paused. "Well, one of the side effects is short-term memory loss. Several of my patients have paid my bill three or four times."

The audience rose and gave him a standing ovation.

DURING THE INTERMISSION AT THE opera, Mrs. Hogan rose from her seat and called, "Is there a doctor in the house? Is there a doctor in the house?"

A man in a tuxedo pushed his way towards her. "I'm a doctor," he said.

"Oh, Doctor," Mrs. Hogan said, "thank goodness you're here. Have I got the loveliest daughter for you . . ."

After just a few years of a marriage filled with constant arguments, a young man and his wife decided that the only way they could save their marriage was through therapy. They had been at each other's throats for some time and felt that they were nearing the final straw.

When the couple arrived at the therapist's office, the therapist jumped right in and opened the floor for discussion. "What seems to be the problem?"

Immediately, the husband held his long face down and didn't say a word. His wife, however, began talking a mile a minute, describing all the wrongs in their marriage:

"He doesn't cook, and when he does, the casserole is always burned. He never remembers to put the cap back on the toothpaste. He always forgets to put the fabric softener in the wash. He stays out late playing poker. He never puts my seat back to the right position after he borrows my car . . ."

After fifteen minutes of listening to the wife, the therapist went over to her, picked her up by her shoulders, kissed her passionately for several minutes, and sat her back down. The wife sat there, absolutely speechless.

He looked over at the husband, who was staring in disbelief at what had happened. The therapist addressed the husband. "Your wife needs that at least twice a week."

The husband scratched his head and replied, "Well, I guess I can have her here on Tuesdays and Thursdays."

AND THEN THERE WAS THE DOCTOR
who was so conceited about his looks and
charm that whenever he took a woman's pulse,
he subtracted ten beats to account for her
being excited to be near him.

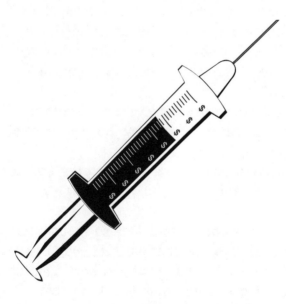

A Texas millionaire had fallen ill. He had consulted many doctors, but not one could figure out what ailed him. Finally, as an incentive, the millionaire let it be known that any doctor who could heal him could have whatever he desired.

A country doctor flew down to Texas and was finally able to diagnose the millionaire. After a week's treatment, he was cured. As the doctor was leaving, the grateful Texan said, "Doc, I am a man of my word. You name it, and, if it is humanly possible, I'll get it for you."

"I really don't need any reward," said the doctor modestly. "This is my job. This is what I love to do."

"No, no—I insist," the Texan protested. "Let me do something—anything—to show my appreciation."

"Well," the doctor said, looking thoughtful, "I guess if it means that much to you. . . . I love to play golf. If I could just have a matching set of golf clubs, that would be great." With that the doctor left.

The doctor didn't hear from the Texan for

some months. Then one day he got a phone call. "Doc, I bet you thought that I had gone back on my word. I have your matching set of golf clubs. The reason it took so long is that I originally didn't think they were good enough for ya. So I had two swimming pools installed and they're all set!"

JOHNNY GOT AN EAR INFECTION AND had to go to the pediatrician, who directed her comments and questions to Johnny in a professional manner. When she asked Johnny, "Is there anything you are allergic to?", he nodded and whispered in her ear.

Smiling, the pediatrician wrote out a prescription and handed it to Johnny's mother. His mother tucked it into her purse without looking at it.

As the pharmacist filled the order, he re-marked on the unusual food-drug interaction precautions Johnny must take. Johnny's mother looked puzzled until he showed her the label on the bottle. Per the doctor's instructions, it read, "Do not take with broccoli."

The patient went to his doctor for a checkup and the doctor wrote out a prescription for him in his usual illegible writing. The patient put it in his pocket, but he forgot to have it filled.

Every morning for two years, he showed it to the conductor as a railroad pass. Twice, it got him into the movies, once into the baseball park, and once into the symphony. He got a raise at work by showing it as a note from the boss.

One day, he mislaid it. His daughter picked it up, played it on the piano, and won a scholarship to a conservatory of music.

A PROFESSOR WATCHED WHILE A mechanic removed engine parts from his car to get to the valves. A surgeon, waiting for his car to be repaired, walked over to observe the process. After they introduced themselves, the two professionals began a conversation and the talk turned to their lines of work.

"You know, Doctor," the professor said, "I sometimes believe this type of work is as complicated as the work we do."

"Perhaps," the surgeon replied. "But let's see him do it while the engine is running."

The young Southern belle came to the hospital for a checkup.

"Have you ever been X-rayed?" asked the doctor.

"Nope," she replied. "But ah've been ultra-violated."

TWO MEN, STEVE AND JOE, WERE IN A hot-air balloon. They drifted into a dense cloudbank and were stuck there for hours. They finally emerged and looked around at the ground below in the hopes of figuring out their location. Suddenly they spotted a man in a garden and shouted down to him.

"Hello down there! Can you tell us where we are?"

The man below looked up and yelled, "You're in a hot-air balloon."

Another cloud came by and engulfed them in its mist. Steve looked at his partner and muttered, "Just our luck, a psychologist."

"Why do you say that?" Joe asked.

"Well, what he said was obviously true, but it didn't help a bit."

Sam was suffering from a miserable cold and went to see his doctor. The doctor prescribed some pills, but they didn't help. On his next visit, the doctor gave him a shot, but that didn't do any good either. On his third visit, the doctor told Sam to go home and take a hot bath. As soon as he was finished bathing, he was to throw open all the windows and stand in the draft.

"But, Doc," Sam protested, "if I do that, I'll get pneumonia."

"I know," said the doctor. "I can cure pneumonia."

MY DOCTOR IS A MAGICIAN. EVERY TIME he sees me, $100 disappears from my pockets and appears in his bill.

Sheri, the pert and pretty nurse, took her troubles to a resident psychiatrist in the hospital where she worked.

"Doctor, you must help me," she pleaded. "It's gotten so that every time I date one of the young doctors here, I end up sleeping with him. Then afterward, I feel guilty and depressed for a week."

"I see," nodded the psychiatrist. "And you, no doubt, want me to strengthen your will power and resolve in this matter."

"No!" exclaimed Sheri. "I want you to fix it so I won't feel guilty and depressed afterward!"

A BIG-SHOT BUSINESSMAN, MR. ROBBINS, had to spend a couple of days in the hospital. He was a royal pain to the nurses and bossed them around, just like he did his employees.

No one on the hospital staff wanted to have anything to do with him.

The head nurse, Nurse Pickens, was the only one who could deal with this patient. She walked into his room and announced, "Mr. Robbins, I have to take your temperature."

After complaining for several minutes, he finally settled down, crossed his arms, and opened his mouth.

"No, I'm sorry," Nurse Pickens stated, "but for this reading, I can't use an oral thermometer."

This started another round of complaining, but eventually Mr. Robbins rolled over and bared his behind.

After feeling the nurse insert the thermometer, he heard her announce, "I have to get something. Now *don't move* until I get back!"

Nurse Pickens left the door to his room open on her way out. Mr. Robbins cursed under his breath as he heard people walking past his door, laughing. After almost an hour, his doctor entered the room.

"What's going on here?" asked the doctor.

THE BEST DOCTOR JOKES EVER

Angrily, Mr. Robbins answered, "What's the matter, Doc? Haven't you ever seen someone having their temperature taken before?"

After a pause, the doctor replied, "Yes, but never with a daffodil!"

A mother was admitted into the hospital for a routine procedure. On her first day out of surgery she learned of the rule stating that children under twelve were prohibited from visiting patients.

Her eleven-year-old daughter seemed to understand, but her six-year-old took the restriction very hard. The mother finally discovered why her daughter was so unusually upset when she was speaking with her on the phone from the hospital for the first time. As her daughter said goodbye, she tearfully exclaimed, "I'll see you when I'm twelve, Mom!"

LARRY WAS IN DR. FEELGOOD'S OFFICE for his annual check-up.

"You won't live out the week," cautioned the

doctor, "if you don't stop running around after women."

"But Doc, there is nothing the matter with me," said Larry, pounding his chest with his fist. "I'm in great physical shape."

"Yes, I know," replied Dr. Feelgood. "But one of the women is my wife."

THE BEST DOCTOR JOKES EVER

A hurricane blew across the Caribbean. It didn't take long for the expensive yacht to be swamped by high waves, sinking without a trace. There were only two survivors: the boat's owner, Dr. Eskin, and its steward, Benny, who managed to swim to the closest island.

After reaching the deserted strip of land, the steward was crying and very upset at the thought that they would never be found. The other man was quite calm, relaxing against a tree.

"Dr. Eskin, Dr. Eskin, how can you be so calm?" cried Benny. "We're going to die on this lonely island. We'll never be discovered here!"

"Sit down and listen to what I have to say, Benny," began the confident Dr. Eskin. "Five years ago I gave the United Way $500,000 and another $500,000 to the United Jewish Appeal. I donated the same amount four years ago. And three years ago, since I did very well in the stock market, I contributed $750,000 to each charity. Last year business was so good that the two charities got a million dollars each!"

"So what?" asked the bewildered Benny.

"Well, it's time for their annual fund drives, and I know they're going to find me."

FRANK WAS SUFFERING FROM A miserable toothache. He was terrified of the dentist, but when the pain became unbearable he gathered up enough nerve to pay him a visit. However, once Frank sat in the chair and saw the drills and wires and other painful-looking implements, he became panicked. The dentist, used to cases like these, asked his assistant to get Frank a bit of whiskey.

"Got your courage back now?" asked the dentist.

"No," Frank replied, trembling.

So a second tot was brought, and then a third.

"Now, have you got your courage?" questioned the dentist.

Frank squared his shoulder and clenched his teeth. "I would like to see the man," he said, "who would *dare* touch my teeth."

At a big cocktail party, an obstetrician's wife noticed that another guest—a big, overly-sexed woman—was making overtures to her husband. But it was a large, informal gathering, so the wife tried to laugh it off. Suddenly, she saw them disappear into a bedroom together.

At once she rushed into the room and pulled the two apart. "Listen lady!" she screamed. "My husband just delivers babies. He doesn't *install* them!"

OVER A ROUND OF GOLF, TWO DOCTORS were talking shop.

"I operated on Mr. Lee the other day," said the surgeon.

"What for?" asked his colleague.

"About $6,000."

"What did he have?"

"About $6,000."

I t is a good idea to shop around before you settle on a doctor. Ask about the condition of his Mercedes. Ask about the competence of his mechanic. Don't be shy! After all, you're paying for it.

—Dave Barry

MR. CURTIS VISITED HIS DOCTOR complaining about a pain in his leg that wouldn't go away. The doctor checked out Curtis's leg, but couldn't find anything wrong. So he gave his patient a full physical exam and ran a gamut of tests, but still couldn't come up with any possible explanation for the pain.

After the exam, the doctor sat Curtis down in his office and said, "I'm sorry, but the pain in your leg is simply caused by old age. There is nothing I can do about it."

Curtis replied with a look of disbelief. "That's impossible! That can't be!"

"What do you mean?" the doctor said, astonished. "I'm the expert here—if you know so much, how can you say that it's *not* old age?"

"Well, I'm no doctor," Curtis answered, "but

it doesn't take a medical degree to tell that your diagnosis is wrong. Clearly, you're mistaken. After all, my other leg feels just fine."

"So what?" said the doctor. "What difference does that make?"

"Well, it doesn't hurt a bit, and it's the same age!"

H arriet had just undergone a very complicated operation. She was feeling better after a few days, except for a bump on her head and a terrible headache. Since it had been an intestinal operation, there was no reason why she should be complaining of a headache.

Finally, Harriet's nurse, fearing that Harriet might be suffering from post-operative shock, spoke to the doctor about it.

"Don't worry about a thing," the doctor assured her. "She really does have a bump on her head. About halfway through the operation we ran out of anesthetic."

OLD DR. CARVER STILL MADE HOUSE calls. One afternoon he was called to the Tuttle house, as Mrs. Tuttle was in terrible pain.

The doctor came out of the bedroom a minute after he'd gone in and asked Mr. Tuttle, "Do you have a hammer?"

A puzzled Mr. Tuttle went out to the garage and returned with a hammer. The doctor thanked him and returned to the bedroom.

A moment later, he came out and asked, "Do you have a chisel?" Mr. Tuttle complied with the request.

In the next ten minutes, Dr. Carver asked for and received a pair of pliers, a screwdriver, and a hacksaw. The final request was the last straw for Mr. Tuttle. "What are you doing to my wife?" he cried.

"Not a thing," replied Dr. Carver. "I can't get my instrument bag open!"

Stanley went to his doctor complaining of recurring chest pains.

After a thorough examination, the doctor escorted Stanley into his office. "Well, there are two divergent opinions on how best to treat you. I'm convinced you need a triple bypass. Your HMO says all you need to do is rub this fourteen-dollar tube of salve on your chest."

A PSYCHOLOGY PROFESSOR AND A DOCTOR were sitting on the porch of a nudist colony, watching the sun set.

The psychologist turned to the doctor. "Have you read Marx?"

The doctor replied, "Yes. I think they are from the wicker chairs."

Dr. Williams recently had a patient drop in on him for an unscheduled appointment. "What can I do for you today?" the doctor asked.

The aged gentleman groaned. "Doctor, you must help me. Every time I make love to my wife, my eyes get all bleary, my legs go weak, and I can hardly catch my breath. Doc, I'm scared!"

Dr. Williams, looking at his 86-year-old patient, soothingly replied, "I wouldn't worry about it. These sensations tend to happen over time, especially to a man of your advanced years. Tell me, when did you first notice these symptoms?"

"Three times last night and twice again this morning!"

DOES AN APPLE A DAY KEEP THE DOCTOR away?

If you aim it well enough.

A woman visited a psychiatrist and begged, "You have to help me, Doctor. My husband thinks he's a racehorse. He neighs, sleeps on straw, and even eats grain!"

"Well, that's a new one," responded the psychiatrist, trying to stifle a snicker. "Nonetheless, I should be able to help him. But I'm going to warn you—it's going to be costly!"

"Oh, money isn't an issue," said the frustrated wife. "He's already won two races."

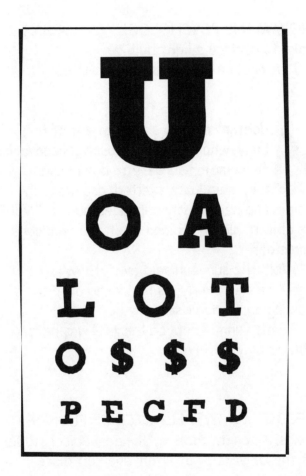

HOW MANY PSYCHOLOGISTS DOES IT take to replace a light bulb?

Just one, but it takes twenty visits.

A doctor came to see a patient of his, Lucy, who was in the hospital recovering from major surgery to both hands.

"Doctor," said Lucy excited, dramatically holding up her heavily bandaged hands. "Will I be able to play the piano when the bandages come off?"

"Well, the surgeon said everything went well," he said slowly, as he looked over the bandaging. "I don't see why not."

"That's funny," replied Lucy. "I was never able to play before."

DEBBIE WAS REALLY SICK OF BLONDE jokes. As an attractive, blonde medical student at the University of Utah, she felt disre-spected—as though Utah natives considered her a blonde beach bimbo. Debbie decided to test her hypothesis. She dyed her hair dark black, and then went to a new area on the medical school grounds to see if people treated her differently.

She saw a farmer unloading a truckload of sheep for the artificial heart program. "You know, I'm a medical student," Debbie said smugly.

The farmer just nodded.

"I'm quite smart," she continued.

The farmer smiled. "I'm sure you are."

"Let me prove it," said Debbie. "Are they paying you for these sheep by the pound?"

"Yep," the farmer replied. "They've budgeted 3,000 bucks. We have to weigh them to see how many I leave here."

"Well, I'll bet you 100 bucks I can calculate in my head how many sheep that is."

The farmer leaned back and pursed his lips. "Well, I don't have 100 bucks on me, but I'll bet a sheep against your hundred."

Debbie studied the flock as it milled around the pen. "Thirty-seven!" she finally yelled triumphantly. "It will take thirty-seven sheep."

Much to Debbie's delight, when the weighing

was complete, the medical school had purchased thirty-seven sheep.

"Well, a bet's a bet," said the farmer. "Go pick a sheep from the rest of the flock."

Debbie ran into the flock and grabbed a fluffy black-and-white one. Holding it with both arms, she walked to her car. She heard the farmer call after her.

"Hey, we farmers are pretty smart, too."

"I'm sure you are," Debbie called back as she continued to her car.

"Let me prove it," the farmer asked, running up to her. "If I can calculate the original color of your hair, can I have my dog back?"

A man goes into a drug store and asks the pharmacist to give him something that would cure hiccups. The pharmacist promptly reached out and slapped the man's face.

"What did you do that for?" the man asked angrily.

"Well, you don't have the hiccups anymore, do you?"

"No," the man shouted, "but my wife out in the car still does!"

AN ANESTHESIOLOGIST IS A DOCTOR who works in the operating room to delay your pain until such time as you get his bill.

Mrs. Porter had been seeing the psychoanalyst for years, pouring her heart out to him twice a week. However, she was making no progress, and the doctor didn't believe she ever would.

"Mrs. Porter," he said at the end of one session, "we've been meeting two times a week for five years now. Do you think these visits are doing you *any* good?"

"Not really," she replied, her voice trembling. "My inferiority complex is as strong as ever."

"Mrs. Porter," the doctor said confidentially, "I have something to tell you. You don't have an inferiority complex. You are, in fact, inferior."

THE DOCTOR HAD JUST COMPLETED HIS examination of a gorgeous red-headed beauty.

"I would suggest to you, young lady, that you discontinue some of your running around," began the medic, as he tried to regain some of his professional dignity. "Stop drinking so much, cut down on your smoking, and above all, start eating properly and getting to bed early."

Then, as a pleasant afterthought, he added, "In fact, why not have dinner with me tonight? I'll see to it that you have the proper food and you'll be in bed by nine o' clock!"

A nurse was leaving the hospital one evening when she found the doctor standing in front of a shredder with a piece of paper in his hand.

"Listen," said the doctor, "this is important and my assistant has left. Any way you can make this thing work?"

"Certainly," replied the nurse, flattered that the doctor had asked for her help. She turned the machine on, inserted the paper, and pressed the start button.

"Excellent! Excellent!" said the doctor as his paper disappeared inside the machine. "I need two copies of that."

MR. AND MRS. SMITH WERE SHOWN INTO the dentist's office, where Mr. Smith made it clear to the dentist that he didn't want to spend a lot of money.

"No fancy stuff, Dr. Morris," Mr. Smith ordered. "No gas or needles of any of that stuff. Just pull the tooth and get it over with."

"I wish more of my patients were as stoic as you," said Dr. Morris admiringly. "Now, which tooth is it?"

Mr. Smith turned to his wife. "Show him your tooth, honey!"

An agitated patient was stomping around the psychiatrist's office, running his hands through his hair and almost in tears.

"Doctor, my memory's gone. Gone! I can't remember my wife's name. Can't remember my children's names. Can't remember what kind of car I drive. Can't remember where I work. It was all I could do to find my way here."

"Calm down. How long have you been like this?"

"Like what?"

I WENT TO MY DOCTOR LAST WEEK WITH a broken arm. I told him that I broke it in two places. His only reply was, "Never go to either of them again."

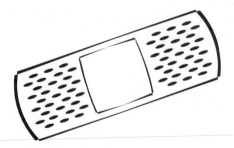

L ouie went to a psychiatrist. "Doc," he said, "I've got trouble. Every time I get into bed, I think there's somebody under it. I get under the bed, I think there's somebody on top of it. Over, under, over, under. You gotta help me, Doc—I'm going crazy!"

"Just put yourself in my hands for two years," said the psychiatrist. "Come to me three times a week, and I'll cure your fears."

"How much do you charge?" Louie asked.

"One hundred dollars a visit."

"I'll sleep on it," Louie replied, and he walked out of the office.

Six months later the psychiatrist met Louie on the street. "Why didn't you ever come to see me again?" he asked.

"For a hundred bucks a visit? A bartender cured me for ten dollars!"

"Is that so? How?"

"He told me to cut the legs off the bed!"

THE RESIDENT DOCTOR WAS PEACEFULLY sleeping when a nurse called her at 3:00 A.M.

"Come quick," she said. "Your patient, Mrs. Dandy, just swallowed a thermometer."

The resident doctor hung up the phone and frantically searched in the dark for her white coat. She was lacing up her shoes when the phone rang again. It was the nurse.

"Never mind," she said. "I found another one."

Peggy injured her leg while skiing one weekend. By the time she got home Saturday, the leg was swollen and she was having difficulty walking, so she had her physician paged. He called Peggy back and told her to soak the leg in hot water.

She tried the hot water, but the leg only became more swollen and painful. Peggy's maid saw her limping and said, "I don't know—I am only a maid—but I always thought it was better to use cold water, not hot, for swelling." Peggy tried switching to cold water and the swelling rapidly subsided.

On Sunday afternoon, she again had the doctor paged so she could complain. "Say, what kind of doctor are you? You told me to soak my leg in hot water and it got worse. It was my maid, for crying out loud, who told me to use cold water. It was fine after that!"

"Really?" answered the doctor. "I don't understand it; *my* maid said to use *hot* water."

BUDDY CALLED HIS DOCTOR TO TELL HIM that his wife, Lorraine, had laryngitis.

"Well, I'm sorry, but in this case, time is the best medicine. There is really nothing I can do to cure your wife's laryngitis."

"Cure it?" Buddy exclaimed. "I want to prolong it!"

A physician presented her bill to the court as the legal way to collect her fees from the deceased person's estate.

"Do you need me to swear to my bill?" the doctor asked of the clerk.

"No," answered the clerk. "Death of the deceased is sufficient evidence that you attended to him professionally."

A FELLOW WALKED INTO A DOCTOR'S office and the receptionist asked him what he had.

"Shingles," he said.

She took down his name, address, and medical insurance number, and told him to have a seat.

A few minutes later a nurse's aid came out and asked him what he had.

"Shingles," he said.

She took down his height, weight, a complete medical history, and told him to wait in the examining room.

Ten minutes later a nurse came in and asked him what he had.

"Shingles," he said.

She gave him a blood test, a blood pressure test, and an electrocardiogram, then told him to take off his clothes and wait for the doctor.

Fifteen minutes later the doctor came in and asked him what he had.

"Shingles," he said.

"Where?" the doctor asked.

"Outside in the truck. Where do you want them?"

H arold went to his doctor complaining that he was no longer able to do all the things around the house that he used to do.

His doctor ran the usual gamut of tests. When the examination was complete, Harold said, "Now, Doc, give it to me straight. I can take it. Just tell me, in plain English, what is wrong with me."

"Well, in plain English," his doctor replied, "you're just plain lazy."

Harold paused. "Okay," he said. "Now give me the medical term so I can tell my wife."

AT THEIR MONTHLY MEETING, THE HEAD doctors in an insane asylum decided that one of their patients was potentially ready for release into the outside world. The doctors wanted to give him a final test, so they decided to escort him to the movies.

When they arrived at the movie theater, they saw "Wet Paint" signs posted above the benches. The doctors knew by touch that the benches were dry, so they just sat down, but the patient put a newspaper down first. The doctors became excited at the prospect that their patient was finally in touch with reality again.

They asked their patient, "Why did you put the newspaper down first?"

"So I'd be higher and have a better view," he replied.

G reg won the lotto for $1 million. But, before he had a chance to hear the happy news, he suffered a heart attack and was admitted into the intensive care unit of the nearby hospital.

Relatives who heard the news were both worried and ecstatic. They wanted to tell Greg of his winnings, but were having trouble figuring out the way to tell him the news without giving him another heart attack. They finally decided to have Greg's doctor tell him, figuring that he would be best able to handle any problems that may suddenly occur from the shock.

The doctor went to Greg's bedside and tried

to think of a delicate way to approach the subject. He finally started with, "Greg, I have an important question to ask you. What would you do if you won a million dollars?"

Greg, sleepy and slightly drugged from medication, replied, "I would give you half of it."

The doctor fainted.

A BUSY SURGEON RETURNED FROM A TWO-week hunting trip complaining angrily to his wife.

"I was there for two weeks. Two weeks! And I didn't kill a damn thing!"

"Well darling," she soothed, "that's what you get for neglecting your practice."

Doctor, Doctor, you've got to help me—I just can't stop my hands from shaking!"

"Do you drink a lot?"

"Not really—I spill most of it!"

M r. Chilton," Dr. Rich said, "I think this will be your last visit."

"Does that mean I'm cured?" he asked.

"For all practical purposes, yes," she replied. "I think we can safely say that your kleptomania is under control. You haven't stolen anything in two years, and we seem to have discovered where your kleptomania stems from. You can look forward to a happy, mentally healthy life."

"Well, that's terrific, Dr. Rich. Before I go, though, I'd like to tell you something. Although our relationship is strictly professional, it's been one of the most rewarding of my life. I wish I could do something to repay you for helping me."

"You've paid my fee," Dr. Rich said. "That's the only responsibility you have."

"I know," Chilton replied. "But I want to do more. Isn't there some kind of personal favor I could do for you?"

"Well," she said, "I'll tell you what. If you ever suffer a relapse, my son could use a nice portable color television."

SHORTLY AFTER THE 911 EMERGENCY number became available, an elderly and quite ill lady appeared in a hospital emergency room, having driven herself to the hospital. She barely managed to stagger in from the parking lot. The horrified nurse rushed over to her with a wheelchair. "Why didn't you call 911 and get an ambulance?"

The lady replied, "My phone doesn't have an eleven."

Lynn was in the hospital recovering from major surgery. She hated being stuck in the tiny little room all day, and to make matters worse, the daily routine was starting to get to her. Every morning, for example, the nurse would bring her breakfast, which invariably consisted of an egg, a piece of toast, and a glass of apple juice. The nurse would then return a little bit later to empty the urine bottle. This same routine had been going on for days.

Finally, one morning Lynn decided to have a little fun. She ate the eggs and the toast, but went to the bathroom where she cleaned out the urine bottle and then poured the apple juice into it. When the nurse returned later that morning, he took a look at the bottle and a frown came over his face.

"Obviously, you enjoyed your breakfast, but something must be wrong. This looks a little cloudy," he said, pointing to the urine bottle.

"Oh really?" she replied, picking up the bottle in question and putting it to her lips. "In that case, we'd better run it through again."

THREE DOCTORS WERE IN A DUCK BLIND and a bird flew overhead. The general practitioner looked at it and said, "Looks like a duck. Flies like a duck. It's probably a duck." He shot at it, but missed, and the bird flew away.

The next bird flew overhead. The pathologist looked at it, then consulted the pages of a
bird manual. "Hmm," he said. "Green wings, yel-
low bill, quacking sound . . . might be a duck."
He raised his gun to shoot it, but the bird was
long gone.

A third bird flew over. The surgeon raised
his gun and shot the bird without even looking.
He turned to the pathologist and said, "Go see
if that was a duck."

A doctor had been having an affair with
his nurse for many months when she
suddenly announced that she was pregnant. Not wanting his wife to know, the doctor
gave the nurse a large sum of money and sent
her to Italy to have the baby.

"How will I let you know when the baby is
born?" she asked.

"Just send me a postcard and write
'spaghetti' on the back," he replied. "I'll take
care of expenses." Heartbroken and having no
other recourse, the nurse took the money and
flew to Italy.

Six months went by, and then one day the doctor's wife called him at the office. "Dear, you received a very strange postcard in the mail today from Italy. I don't quite understand what it means."

The doctor, suddenly racked with guilt, said, "Just wait until I get home—I will explain everything to you then."

The doctor came home later that evening, read the postcard, and fell to the floor with a heart attack. Paramedics rushed him to the hospital emergency room, and the head medic stayed back to comfort his wife. The medic asked what trauma, if any, had precipitated the cardiac arrest.

"I don't know," the wife sobbed. "All he did was read a postcard. I didn't even understand what it said: 'Spaghetti, spaghetti, spaghetti, spaghetti—two with sausage and meatballs, two without.'"

TWO PSYCHIATRISTS, DR. SIMMONS AND Dr. Johnson, were at a convention. As they talked shop over a drink, Simmons said, "So tell me. What was your most difficult case?"

Johnson replied, "I had a patient who lived in a pure fantasy world. He believed that an uncle in South America was going to die and leave him a fortune. All day long he waited for a letter to arrive from an attorney. He never went out, he never did anything—he merely sat around and waited for this fantasy letter from this fantasy uncle."

"What was the result?" Simmons asked.

"It was an eight-year struggle. I worked with this patient every day for eight years, but I finally cured him. Then that stupid letter arrived!"

Nancy, still woozy from surgery, heard Dr. Williams as he leaned over her in the hospital bed.

"We've operated on your eyes and were able to save one of them," he announced.

"Oh, thank you," murmured Nancy. "That's wonderful."

"Yes," Dr. Williams replied. "We'll give it to you on your way out."

A FATHER BROUGHT HIS SON TO THE doctor after the boy had shoved a toy car up his nose. As the doctor tried to remove the car, the incredulous father kept repeating, "I don't know how he did it! I have no idea how he did it!" Finally, the doctor dislodged the toy, and father and son happily left the office.

A few hours later, the father came back with the toy shoved up his nose. When the doctor walked in the room, all he said was, "I know how he did it!"

A patient complained to his doctor, "I've been to three other doctors and none of them agreed with your diagnosis." The doctor calmly replied, "Just wait until the autopsy. Then they'll see that I was right."

DID YOU HEAR THE ONE ABOUT THE YOUNG
bone specialist?

He just opened his office and only needed a
good break to get started.

A first-time mother went into labor late one evening, and she and her husband rushed to the hospital. Upon their arrival, her doctor said he had invented a new machine that would transfer a portion of the mother's labor pain to the father. He asked if they were willing to try it out. The father, being the sensitive man that he was, was very much in favor of relieving his wife of some of her pain.

The doctor initially set the knob to ten percent, explaining that even ten percent was probably more pain than the father had ever experienced before. But as labor progressed, the husband felt fine, so he asked the doctor to go ahead and bump it up a notch. The doctor adjusted the machine to twenty percent.

The husband was still feeling fine. The doctor checked the husband's blood pressure and pulse and was amazed at how well he was doing. At this, they decided to try for fifty percent.

The husband continued to have no trouble. Since it was obviously helping out his wife considerably, he encouraged the doctor to transfer *all* the pain to him. The wife delivered a healthy baby with virtually no pain. She and her husband were ecstatic.

When they got home, they found the mailman dead on their porch.

LUCY WENT TO HER DOCTOR LATE ONE night, complaining of severe pain. "You have to help me," she moaned. "I hurt all over."

"What do you mean 'all over'?" asked the doctor. "You have to be a little more specific."

Lucy touched her right knee with her index finger and yelled, "Ow, that hurts." Then she touched her left cheek. "Ouch! That hurts, too!" Then she touched her right earlobe. "Yow—even *that* hurts," she wailed.

The doctor began his exam, but after only two minutes was able to tell her his diagnosis: "You have a broken finger."

L ate one night the doctor was called to the hospital for an emergency, and he left his wife home alone. Suddenly, the doorbell rang.

"Is the doctor at home?" asked the man at the door, in a very hoarse and quiet voice due to his aching throat.

"No, come on in!" whispered the doctor's wife in return.

DOCTOR: DID YOU TAKE THE PATIENT'S temperature?
Nurse: No. Is it missing?

C handler wasn't too happy with his doctor's recommendation to cure his constant fatigue.

"You want me to give up sex completely, Doc?" he cried. "I'm a young guy. I'm in the prime of my life. How do you expect me to give up sex and go cold turkey?"

"Well," replied the doctor, "you could get married and taper off gradually."

THE BEST DOCTOR JOKES EVER

A PSYCHIATRIST VISITED A MENTAL institution and asked a patient, "How did you get here? What was the nature of your illness?"

He received this reply: "Well, it all started when I got married. I guess I should never have done it. I got hitched to a widow with a grown daughter who then became my stepdaughter. My daddy came to visit us, fell in love with my lovely stepdaughter, then married her. And so my stepdaughter was now my stepmother. Soon, my wife had a son who was, of course, my daddy's brother-in-law since he is the half-brother of my stepdaughter, who is now, of course, my daddy's wife. So, as I told you, when my stepdaughter married my daddy, she was at once my stepmother!

"Now, since my new son is brother to my stepmother, he also became my uncle. As you know, my wife is my step-grandmother since she is my stepmother's mother. Don't forget that my stepmother is my stepdaughter. Remember, too, that I am my wife's grandson. But hold on just a few minutes more. You see, since I'm married to my step-grandmother, I

---

am not only the wife's grandson and her hubby, but I am also my own grandfather.

"Now can you understand how I got put in this place?"

I'm afraid I have some very bad news," the doctor said. "You're dying, and you don't have much time left."

"Oh, that's terrible," cried his patient. "How long have I got?"

"Ten," the doctor said sadly.

"Ten?" the patient asked. "Ten what? Months? Weeks? What?"

"Nine . . ."

A VISITOR WAS ABOUT TO ENTER THE hospital when he saw two white-coated doctors searching through the flower beds.

"Excuse me," he said. "Have you lost something?"

"No," replied one of the doctors. "We're doing a heart transplant for an income-tax inspector and want to find a suitable stone."

Diane went to the doctor and complained that her husband was losing interest in sex. The doctor gave her a pill, but warned her that it was still experimental and to take care where and how she used it. That night at dinner, Diane slipped it into her husband's mashed potatoes.

About a week later she was back at the doctor, absolutely ecstatic. "Doc, the pill worked great! I put it in my husband's potatoes, and it wasn't five minutes before he jumped up, raked all the food and dishes onto the floor, and grabbed me around the waist. Before I knew it, he was ripping off all my clothes and ravaging me right there on the table!"

"My goodness! I'm so sorry," the doctor said apologetically. "We didn't realize the pill was that strong! The foundation will be glad to pay for any damages."

"Nah, that's okay," Diane said. "We weren't planning on going back to that restaurant anyway."

DR. SAMSON HAD BEEN ATTENDING TO A rich old man for some time, but it became apparent that the old chap didn't have much longer to live. Accordingly, the doctor advised his wealthy patient to put his affairs in order.

"Oh, yes, I've done that," said the old gentleman. "I've only got to make a will. And do you know what I'm going to do with all my money? I'm going to leave it to the doctor who saves my life."

THE BEST DOCTOR JOKES EVER

A pretty young woman, visiting her new doctor for the first time, found herself alone in a small examining room. She began undressing nervously, preparing herself for the upcoming examination. Just as she draped the last of her garments over the back of a chair, a light rap sounded on the door and a young doctor strode in.

Coming to an abrupt halt, the doctor looked his nude patient up and down carefully and with considerable appreciation.

"Well, Miss James," he said finally, "it seems obvious to me that until today you have never undergone an eye examination."

CHRIS WENT TO SEE HIS DOCTOR AND asked him if he would live to be a hundred.

"Well, there are some easy ways to judge," said the doctor. "Do you smoke or drink?"

"No," Chris replied. "I've never done either."

"Do you gamble?"

"Nope."

"Drive fast cars?"

Chris shook his head.

The doctor leaned over confidentially. "Fool around with any women?" he said, with a little grin.

Chris shook his head sadly. "No, Doc—never."

"Well then," cried the doctor. "What do you want to live to be a hundred for?"

I'm sorry, ma'am, but I have to charge you $100 for pulling your boy's tooth."

"One hundred dollars! Why, I understood you to say that you charged only $20 for such work!"

"That's true," replied the dentist. "But this youngster yelled so terribly that he scared four other patients out of the office!"

"THE DOCTOR SAID HE WOULD HAVE ME on my feet in two weeks."

"Was he successful?"

"Yup. I had to sell my car to pay his bill."

DOCTOR: YOU NEED GLASSES.
  Patient: But I'm wearing glasses, Doc.
  Doctor: Then I need glasses.

An old couple, George and Myrtle, were waiting to see the doctor. George was called in first for his physical, and once the doctor had finished, he sent George back into the waiting room and called for Myrtle.

"Before we proceed with the examination, I would like to have a quick word with you about your husband," said the doctor.

"Oh no, it's his heart, isn't it?" Myrtle said.

"No, no. Physically, George is doing just fine," the doctor replied. "It's his mental state that I'm concerned about."

"What do you mean?" Myrtle asked.

"Well, I asked him how he was feeling and he told me he felt great. Then he said that when he gets up at night to go to the bathroom, he opens the door and God turns on the light for him. When he's finished, he shuts the door and God turns the light off."

"Son of a gun!" Myrtle cried. "The old fool's been peeing in the fridge again!"

A child psychologist, working for the local elementary school, was asked to see a pupil who drew all his pictures with black and brown crayons. She talked to him, but saw nothing obvious in his responses. She gave him projective tests, but saw nothing conclusive in the results.

Finally, in desperation, she gave him some paper and a new box of crayons.

"Oh, goody!" said the boy. "I got an old box in school and only the black and brown ones are left."

JOHNSON WENT TO HIS DOCTOR AND told him that he hadn't been feeling well lately. The doctor examined him, left the room, and came back with three different bottles of pills.

The doctor gave Johnson his instructions: "Take the green pill with a big glass of water when you wake up. Take the blue pill with a big glass of water after you eat lunch. Then just before going to bed, take the red pill with another big glass of water."

Startled to be put on so much medicine, Johnson stammered, "Jeez, Doc, exactly what is my problem?"

The doctor replied, "You're not drinking enough water."

A DOCTOR TOLD A BOY, "THIS INJECTION won't hurt a bit."

Now *that's* an MD promise.

Old Mrs. Grumblebum went every day to visit her doctor. The doctor—a very patient man—humored her, listened quietly, and sometimes even prescribed medication. One day Mrs. Grumblebum didn't show up.

The next day the doctor asked, "Where were you yesterday? I missed you."

"I'll tell you the truth," Mrs. Grumblebum replied, "I was sick!"

A new patient was quite upset when a nurse led him to a small, curtained cubicle and told him to undress. "But I only want the doctor to look at an ingrown toenail!" he protested.

"Our rule is that everyone must undress," replied the nurse as she handed him a very skimpy johnny.

"That's a stupid rule," grumbled the patient. "Making me undress just to look at my toe."

"That's nothing," growled a voice from the next cubicle. "I just came to fix the phones!"

CASEY RETURNED FROM THE DOCTOR looking very worried. His wife, immediately concerned, said, "Oh, no. What is it?"

Casey replied, "The doctor told me I have to take a pill every day for the rest of my life."

"Oh," his wife sighed, relieved. "Is that all? Many people have to take pills daily."

"I know," Casey cried, "but he only gave me four pills!"

Following Thomson's physical, Dr. Munro sent his patient a bill. When a month went by without a remittance, Dr. Munro sent another bill, and then a third, and then a fourth, but to no avail. Finally he sent Thomson a pathetic letter, claiming desperately strained circumstances and enclosing a shot of his infant daughter. On the back of the snapshot he scribbled, "The reason I need the money you owe me!"

Barely a week later a response from Thomson arrived in the mail. Dr. Munro eagerly ripped it open, and found himself holding a picture of a gorgeous woman in a mink coat. On the back of the photograph the patient had scrawled, "The reason I can't pay!"

SAL WENT TO THE DOCTOR COMPLAINING of terrible migraines. "I can't stand it, Doc," he wailed. "No matter how much medicine I take, the pain doesn't go away!"

"When I have a migraine," replied the doctor, "I go home and soak in a hot bath. Then I have my wife sponge me off with the hottest water I can stand, especially around the fore-head. We go into the bedroom, and even if my head is killing me, we have sex. Almost imme-diately, the headache is gone. Try it and come back in six weeks."

Six weeks later, the patient returned with a big grin. "It worked!" he exclaimed. "I've had migraines for three years, and no one's ever helped me before. I feel like I have my life back. I owe you, Doc."

"Glad to help," said the doctor, pleased.

"By the way," the patient added, "you have a really nice house."

Wwhat is the difference between God and an orthopedic surgeon? God doesn't think he's an ortho-pedic surgeon.

SIGN SEEN ON THE DOOR OF A MEDICAL school building: "Staph Only"

Mandy went to the dentist to have her teeth cleaned. While she was there, she commented to him that it must be hard spending all day with your hands in someone's mouth.

"Nah, it's all right," the dentist replied. "I just think of it as having my hands in their wallet."

WHILE ATTENDING A CONVENTION, three psychiatrists took a walk and began to gripe about their shared profession.

"People are always coming to us with their guilt and fears," one said. "We have no one to go to with our own problems."

"Well, here's the perfect opportunity! Since we're all professionals, why don't we hear each other out right now?" another suggested.

All agreed that this was a good idea. The first psychiatrist confessed, "I'm a shopper and deeply in debt, so I usually over-bill my patients as often as I can."

The second admitted, "I have a drug problem that's out of control. I frequently pressure my patients into buying illegal drugs for me."

The third psychiatrist spoke up. "I know it's wrong, but no matter how hard I try, I just can't keep a secret."

A 92-year-old woman fell to the floor, clutching her chest in pain. An ambulance was summoned, and she was in full cardiac arrest by the time the ambulance reached the hospital. After about thirty minutes of unsuccessful resuscitation attempts, the old woman was pronounced dead.

The doctor went into the waiting room to tell the woman's 74-year-old daughter that her mother didn't make it.

"Didn't make it?" the daughter responded. "Where could they be? She left in the ambulance forty-five minutes ago!"

"YOU'RE GOING OUT TO PLAY GOLF AGAIN?" the woman complained.

"I'm only doing as the doctor ordered," her husband replied.

"That's nonsense! Do I look stupid to you?" she cried.

"But it's true," he said, while walking out the door. "He told me specifically that I should get some iron every day."

A short history of medicine: "Doctor, I have an earache."

2000 B.C.: "Here, eat this root."

1000 B.C.: "That root is heathen. Say this prayer."

1850 A.D.: "That prayer is superstition. Drink this potion."

1940 A.D.: "That potion is snake oil. Swallow this pill."

1985 A.D.: "That pill is ineffective. Take this antibiotic."

2000 A.D.: "That antibiotic is artificial. Here, eat this root!"

A PHYSICIAN AND HER FOUR-YEAR-OLD daughter were on the way to drop the daughter off at preschool. On the way there, the little girl picked up the stethoscope that the doctor had left on the car seat and began to play with it.

"Be still my heart!" thought her mother. "My daughter wants to follow in my footsteps!"

Then the child spoke into the instrument. "Welcome to McDonalds. May I take your order?"

A pipe burst in a doctor's house, so he called a plumber. The plumber arrived, unpacked his tools, and did mysterious plumber-type things for a while. He handed the doctor a bill for $600.

The doctor started to rant and rave, "This is ridiculous! Six hundred dollars? I didn't even make that much as a doctor!"

The plumber quietly replied, "Neither did I when I was a doctor."

LITTLE TOMMY: YOU SAID THE SCHOOL dentist would be painless, but he wasn't.

Teacher: Did he hurt you?

Little Tommy: No, but he screamed when I bit his finger.

An old country doctor went out to the boondocks to deliver a baby; in fact it was so far out in the country that there was no electricity. When the doctor arrived, no one was home except for the laboring mother and her five-year-old child.

In spite of the child's young age, the doctor decided to enlist his help. He instructed the young lad to hold a lantern up high so the doctor could see while he helped the woman deliver the baby. The mother pushed and pushed and after a bit, the doctor lifted the newborn baby by the feet and spanked him on the bottom to help him to take his first breath.

The doctor turned to the five-year-old. "So, what do you think of your new baby brother?"

"Spank him again," the five-year-old replied. "He shouldn't have crawled up there in the first place."

THE RESIDENT WALKED IN TO THE ER examining room of a local hospital. He found an elderly man lying on a stretcher.

"Well, now," the resident said, patting the older man on the arm reassuringly, "What brought you to us today?"

"An ambulance," the elderly gentleman replied.

The doctor had just been buried.

The last words of the service over, his bereaved friends and family started towards their cars. They suddenly stopped. A strange, eerie sound was heard from the grave.

As the guests looked around, a colleague of the deceased said, "Don't worry. It's just his pager."

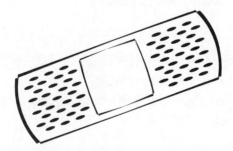

A VERY NERVOUS MAN, ACCOMPANIED BY his nagging wife, was examined by a doctor. After checking the chart, he nodded and wrote the man a prescription for a powerful tranquilizer.

"How often do I take these?" the man asked.

"Let's start off with one every six hours. But they're not for you," replied the doctor. "They're for your wife."

Carla was lying in bed, still groggy from the effects of the recent operation. Her doctor came in, looking very glum.

"I can't be sure what's wrong with you," the doctor said. "I think it's the drinking."

"Okay," Carla replied. "Can we get an opinion from a doctor who's sober?"

HOW MANY PSYCHIATRISTS DOES IT take to change a light bulb?

Only one, but the light bulb has to *want* to change.

A young woman having a physical exam was very embarrassed about her weight problem. As she removed her last bit of clothing, she blushed.

"I'm so ashamed, Doctor," she said. "I guess I let myself go."

The physician checked her eyes and ears. "Don't feel ashamed, Miss. You don't look that bad."

"Do you really think so, Doctor?" she asked.

The doctor held a tongue depressor in front of her face and said, "Of course. Now just open your mouth and say 'Moo.'"

A WELL-RESPECTED CITY DOCTOR WAS tired of his fast-paced, urban lifestyle and decided to set up a practice in a small country town. One of his first house calls was to a farmer who lived in a large farmhouse in the country.

After the doctor visited the farm several times for various family emergencies, the farmer noticed that the doctor was no longer willing to come to the farm. He always insisted that the family come to his office in the case of an illness.

One afternoon, the farmer called the doctor concerned about his daughter, who had a bad fever. Again, the doctor insisted that the farmer bring his daughter to the office. The farmer finally spoke up. "Lookee here, Doc, I seem to recall that you used to come all the time to our neck of the woods. What's the matter—don't yer like us or somethin'?"

"No, no," the doctor insisted. "To be honest, well, it's your ducks at the entrance. Every time I enter the farm, they insult me!"

Three doctors were on their way to a convention when their car got a flat. They got out and examined the tire. The first doctor said, "I think it's flat."

The second doctor examined it closely and agreed. "It sure looks flat."

The third doctor felt the tire. "Mmm, yes. It feels like it's flat."

All three nodded their heads in agreement. "We'd better run some tests."

A MAN WALKED INTO A DOCTOR'S OFFICE. He had a cucumber up his nose, a carrot in his left ear, and a banana in his right ear.

"What's the matter with me?" he asked the doctor.

The doctor replied, "You're not eating properly."

A husband and wife were at their first doctor visit prior to the birth of their new child. After everything checked out, the doctor took a small stamp and stamped something on the mom-to-be's stomach with indelible ink.

The couple was curious about the meaning of the stamp, so when they got home the husband dug out his magnifying glass. In very tiny letters, the stamp said, "When you can read this, come back and see me."

THE OLD FAMILY PHYSICIAN WENT AWAY on vacation and entrusted his practice to his son, a medical student. Upon the physician's return, his son provided him with detailed information of his casework for the week. He was particularly proud that he cured Miss Ferguson, an aged and wealthy spinster, of her chronic indigestion.

"My boy," said the old doctor, "I'm proud of you, but Miss Ferguson's indigestion is what put you through college."

A new nurse listened while Dr. Blake was yelling, "Typhoid! Tetanus! Measles!" The new nurse turned to Nurse Simons, "Why is he doing that?"

She replied, "Oh, he just likes to call the shots around here."

ARNIE WALKED INTO A PSYCHOLOGIST'S office, looking very depressed. "Doc, you've got to help me. I can't go on like this."

"What's the problem?" the psychologist inquired.

"Well, I'm 35 years old and I still have no luck with the ladies. No matter how hard I try, I either scare them away or turn them off somehow."

"My friend, this is not a serious problem," the kindly psychologist said. "You just need to work on your self-esteem. Each morning, I want you to get up and run to the bathroom mirror. Tell yourself that you are a good person, a fun person, and an attractive person. But be sure to say it with real conviction. Within a week you'll have women buzzing all around you." Arnie seemed content with this advice and walked out of the office a bit excited.

Three weeks later he returned with the same downtrodden expression on his face.

"Did my advice not work?" said the psychologist.

"Oh, it worked all right," Arnie replied. "For the past several weeks I've enjoyed some of the best moments of my life with the most fabulous looking women."

"So what's your problem?" asked the psychologist.

"I don't have a problem," Arnie blurted. "My wife does."

An old man went to his doctor for a physical.

"Take off all your clothes," his doctor said. The old man obliged.

"Now go look out that window," the doctor instructed. Again, the old man did as he was told.

"Now stick out your tongue." The old man was confused by now, but he did it anyway. He turned to his doctor and asked, "What did that tell you, Doc?"

"Nothing," the doctor replied. "I'm mad at my neighbor."

AN APPLICANT WAS BEING INTERVIEWED for admission to a prominent medical school. "Tell me," inquired the interviewer, "where do you expect to be in five years?"

"Well, let's see," replied the student. "It's Wednesday afternoon. I guess I'd be on the golf course by now."

I'm treating a patient with a split personality," boasted a psychiatrist, "and Medicare pays for both of them!"

AN EXPECTANT MOTHER WAS BEING rushed to the hospital, but didn't quite make it. She gave birth to her baby on the hospital lawn. A month later, the father received the hospital bill. One of the items on the bill: "Delivery Room Fee: $500."

He wrote the hospital and reminded them that the baby was born on the front lawn. A week passed, and a corrected bill arrived: "Greens Fee: $200."

The surgeon was standing by his patient's bed as he was waking up from surgery.
"I'm afraid we're going to have to operate on you again," he said to his groggy patient. "You see, I left my rubber gloves inside you."

"Well, if that's the only reason, I'd rather pay for the gloves than have you go near me again."

AN ARTIST ASKED THE GALLERY OWNER anyone had shown interest in his paintings.

"Well, yes, as a matter of fact, one man did," she replied.

"Wow! Did he?" the artist asked, impressed with himself. "Well, what did he say?"

"He inquired if your work would appreciate in value after you died. When I told him it would, he bought all fifteen of your paintings. But I also have some bad news."

"Bad news?" the artist said. "It couldn't be all that bad after that great news you had for me."

"The man was your doctor."

N urse: Doctor, Doctor—the man you just treated collapsed on the front step! What should I do?

Doctor: Turn him around so it looks like he was just arriving!

WHAT DO YOU CALL TWO ORTHOPEDIC doctors reading an EKG?

A double blind study.

Helga went to a medical clinic for an electrocardiogram. While the technician was lining up the machine, Helga told her that she had dextrocardia.

"What's that?" the technician asked.

"It means that my heart is on the right side of my chest, rather than on the left," Helga answered. "It's important that you set up your machine to accommodate that."

As the technician attached the wires, she asked casually, "Tell me—have you had that for long?"

A DOCTOR WAS AWAKENED AT FOUR IN the morning by a caller who wanted to know how much the doctor charged for a house call.

"By god, what time is it?" demanded the angry physician. "This better be an emergency. I charge $25."

"How much is an office visit?" asked the caller.

"Fifteen dollars."

"Okay, Doc," said the caller. "I'll meet you in your office in fifteen minutes."

B illy was in the pediatrician's waiting room when he saw another boy his age crying.
"What's the matter?" Billy asked him.
"I'm here for a blood test, and they're going to cut my finger!"
At this, Billy burst into tears.
"Why are *you* crying?" the other boy asked.
"I'm here for a urine test!"

A FATHER WAS MAKING HIS FIRST VISIT to a hospital where his teenage son was about to have an operation. He watched the doctor's every move. As the doctor placed a mask over the son's mouth, the father asked, "What's that?"
The doctor explained, "This is an anesthetic. After he gets this, he won't know a thing."
"Save your time, Doc," exclaimed the father. "He doesn't know a thing now!"

W hile making rounds, a doctor pointed out an X-ray to a group of medical students.

"As you can see," she said, "the patient limps because his left fibula and tibia are radically arched. Michael, what would you do in a case like this?"

"Well," pondered the student, "I suppose I'd limp, too."

A PATIENT WAS IN AT HIS DENTIST FOR a cleaning when the dentist said, "Could you help me out? I'd like you to give a few of your loudest screams."

"But, why?" asked the patient. "It isn't all that bad this time."

The dentist sighed. "I know, but there are about fifteen people in the waiting room right now, and I don't want to miss the ball game at seven o'clock!"

Mr. Smith was brought to Mercy Hospital and quickly taken in for coronary surgery. The operation went well and, as he regained consciousness, a Sister of Mercy was waiting by his bed.

"Mr. Smith, you're going to be just fine," said the nun, gently patting his hand. "We do need to know, however, how you intend to pay for your stay here. Are you covered by insurance?"

"No, I'm not," the man whispered hoarsely.

"Then can you pay in cash?" persisted the nun.

"I'm afraid I cannot, Sister."

"Well, do you have any close relatives?" the nun questioned sternly.

"Just my sister in New Mexico," he volunteered. "But she's a humble spinster nun."

The Sister was a little miffed. "I must correct you, Mr. Smith. Nuns are not spinsters—they are married to God."

"Wonderful," said Mr. Smith. "In that case, please send the bill to my brother-in-law."

A MAN SPOKE FRANTICALLY INTO THE phone. "My wife is pregnant, and her contractions are only two minutes apart!"

"Is this her first child?" the doctor queried.

"No, you *idiot!*" the man shouted. "This is her husband!"

During the peak of the cold and flu season last winter, Dr. Peterson found himself giving a lot of penicillin shots. He decided to tack the following sign to his front door: "To Save Time, Please Back Into the Office."

AFTER A LONG AND SERIOUS OPERATION, Lena ended up in a coma. Try as they might, the doctors just couldn't bring her out of it. When her husband, Ralph, came into the intensive care unit to see her, the doctors gave him the bad news.

"We just can't wake her. It doesn't look good, I'm afraid," the doctor told Ralph in a quiet, somber voice.

Ralph looked at Lena and with a trembling voice said, "But Doctor, she's so young. She's only 45."

"Thirty-seven," came the weak reply from Lena.

Patient: Doctor, what I need is something to stir me up, something to put me in a fighting mood. Did you put something like that in this prescription?

Doctor: No need for that. You'll find that in your bill.

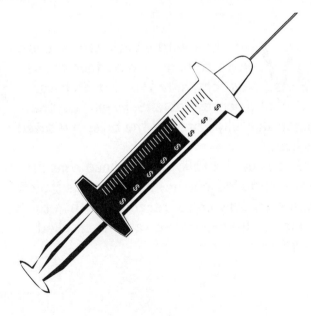

FRED, A 92-YEAR-OLD MAN, HAD JUST
been to the doctor for a physical. A few days
later, his doctor saw him on the street with a
gorgeous young lady on his arm.

"Fred, what do you think you're doing?" his
doctor admonished.

"Why, just what you said, Doc!" Fred
answered. "Get a hot momma and be cheerful!"

"No," the doctor replied, "I said you've got a
heart murmur. Be *careful*."

When the wealthy businessman choked
on a fish bone at a restaurant, he
was fortunate that a doctor was
seated at a nearby table. Springing up, the
doctor skillfully removed the bone and saved
his life.

As soon as the fellow had calmed himself
and could talk again, he thanked the surgeon
enthusiastically and offered to pay him for his
services. "Just name the fee," he croaked
gratefully.

"Okay," replied the doctor. "How about half of what you'd have offered when the bone was still stuck in your throat?"

A WOMAN CAME IN WITH HER HUSBAND and three children for her yearly physical.

After the examination, the doctor took the woman's husband aside. He said, in a low voice, "I don't like the looks of your wife at all."

"Me either, doc," said the husband. "But she's a great cook and really good with the kids."

A doctor wrote about an epitaph he had seen in a local cemetery:

"In memory of my father, gone to join his appendix, his tonsils, his olfactory nerve, a kidney, an eardrum, and a leg prematurely removed by an intern who needed the experience."

AN ANNOYINGLY SELF-RIGHTEOUS MAN went to the doctor for a check-up. "I feel terrible," Horace moaned. "Please examine me and tell me what's wrong!"

"Let's begin with a few questions," said the doctor. "Do you drink much?"

"Alcohol?" said Horace. "I'm a teetotaler. Never touch a drop."

"How about smoking?" asked the doctor.

"Never," Horace gushed. "Tobacco is bad, and I have strong principles against it."

"Well, uh," asked the doctor, "do you have much of a sex life?"

"Absolutely not!" said Horace, horrified. "Sex is a sin. I'm in bed by ten o'clock every night. Always have been."

The doctor paused, looked at Horace hard, and asked, "Do you have pains in your head?"

"Yes, as a matter of fact I do," replied Horace. "In fact, I have terrible pains in my head."

"Well, that's your trouble," said the doctor. "Your halo is on too tight."

A patient called his dentist to inquire about the price of pulling a tooth.

"Two hundred and fifty dollars," the dentist said.

The patient was shocked. "What? Two hundred and fifty dollars for just a few minutes work?"

"I can extract it very slowly if you like."

TWO SURGEONS WERE SITTING OVER coffee in the hospital's cafeteria.

"Yesterday I removed wealthy Mrs. Hollingsworth's appendix," said the surgeon.

"Now the appendix?" said his partner. "Have you discovered what her real problem is?"

The man looked a little worried when the doctor came in to administer his annual physical, so the first thing the doctor did was to ask whether anything was troubling him.

"Well, to tell the truth, Doc, yes," answered the patient. "You see, I seem to be getting forgetful. No, it's actually worse than that. I'm never sure I can remember where I put the car, or whether I answered a letter, or where I'm going, or what it is I'm going to do once I get there—that is, *if* I get there. So I really need your help. What can I do?"

The doctor mused for only one or two beats, then answered in his kindliest tones, "Pay me in advance."

MICKEY AND JENNY WERE TRYING TO figure out what game to play. Mickey suggested, "Let's play doctor."

"Good idea," said Jenny. "You operate, and I'll sue."

A doctor was to give a speech at an AMA dinner. Running late, he quickly jotted down some notes for his speech. Unfortunately, as he stood in front of his colleagues later that night, he found that he couldn't read his notes. He shuffled his notes and nervously cleared his throat as he frantically tried to come up with something to say. Suddenly, his face brightened. "Is there a pharmacist in the house?"

A PATIENT TOLD HIS THERAPIST, "I FEEL like a new man."

The therapist replied, "Well, can this new man afford me?"

A doctor died and went to hell. He was met at the gate and asked to wait for Satan. After four hours, Satan finally appeared.

The doctor was incensed. Poking his watch, he said, "How could you keep me waiting so long! I'm an important man! I'm a doctor!"

"Doctors are a dime a dozen here in hell," Satan replied. "But, I'll tell you what. Since you had to wait so long, I'll give you a choice of which part of hell you will spend eternity in." Satan took the doctor down a hall. "Here. I'll be back shortly. You can choose between Door #1 and Door #2. I'll be back and you can let me know where you want to be assigned."

The doctor opened Door #1. Inside was an Intensive Care Unit. Blood was spurting, alarms were going off, and patients were coding. A man in the corner extubated himself as a woman in the center fell out of bed. The doctor quickly shut the door and decided to check Door #2.

Behind Door #2 was a Medical Records Department. Unfinished charts stretched for miles with notations about delinquent H&Ps.

Message slips from Managed Care Case Managers filled a swimming pool sized bin. Inside, physicians were dictating as sweat poured off their brows. The doctor shut the door and shuddered. "I don't know which one is worse."

Then he noticed another door off to the side. He opened it and inside was a tidy nurses' station. The nurses were all young and beautiful. They were busily making rounds with doctors, and calling to obtain lab and X-ray results. The nurses poured coffee and served donuts purchased with their own money. One doctor complained of a stiff neck and a nurse rubbed it for him. "Now this is more like it," the doctor thought as he closed the door.

Satan came strolling towards him and said, "Well, which have you decided on: Door #1 or Door #2?"

"Actually, I'd like to go behind Door #3," the doctor replied.

"I'm sorry, but that's not an option."

"But that's what I want!" cried the doctor.

"You can't go in there," Satan replied. "That's hell for nurses."

MIKE WENT TO THE DOCTOR AND WHINED, "I have a rash on my arm."

"Does it burn?" asked the doctor.

"I don't know," said Mike. "I never tried to light it."

L ate one night at the insane asylum, an inmate shouted, "I am Napoleon!"

Another inmate asked, "How do you know?"

"God told me!"

A voice from another room suddenly shouted, "I did not!"

"SO, HOW DID IT HAPPEN?" THE DOCTOR asked the middle-aged farmhand as he set the man's broken leg.

"Well, Doc, twenty-five years ago—"

"Never mind the past. Tell me how you broke your leg this morning."

"Like I was saying, Doc. . . . Twenty-five years ago, when I first started working on the farm, that night, right after I'd gone to bed, the farmer's beautiful daughter came into my room. She asked me if there was anything I wanted. I said, no, everything is fine. 'Are you sure?' she asked. 'I'm sure,' I said. 'Isn't there *anything* I can do for you?' she wanted to know. 'I reckon not,' I replied.

"Excuse me," said the doctor, "but what does this story have to do with your leg?"

"Well, this morning," the farmhand explained, "when it dawned on me what she meant, I fell off the roof!"

Little Suzy was taken to the dentist, where it was discovered that she had a cavity that would have to be filled.

"Now, young lady," asked the dentist. "What kind of filling would you like for that tooth?"

"Chocolate, please," replied the youngster.

WHY DO PSYCHIATRISTS GIVE THEIR patients shock treatment?

To prepare them for the bill.

A surgeon was getting ready to operate. "Why are you wearing gloves?" asked his drowsy patient.

The surgeon smiled. "Don't want to leave any fingerprints."

I MUST TELL YOU ABOUT UNCLE HARRY. He was a dentist and he had this approach: for every one tooth he'd extracted from a patient, he took out two of his own. He was a dentist for one week. You don't get that kind of compassion today.

—Arthur Brown

A doctor had a problem with a leak in his bathroom plumbing that only got worse and worse. He finally awoke one night to find a flood in his bathroom. Even though it was 2:00 A.M., the doctor decided to phone his plumber.

"For crying out loud, Doc," his plumber wailed, "this is some time to wake a guy."

"Well," the doctor answered testily, "you've never hesitated to call me in the middle of the night with a medical problem. Now it just happens I've got a plumbing emergency."

There was a moment's silence. Then the plumber spoke up. "Right you are, Doc," he agreed. "Tell me what's wrong."

The doctor explained about the leak in the bathroom. "I'll tell you what you should do," the plumber offered. "Take two aspirins every four hours and drop them down the pipe. If the leak hasn't cleared up by morning, phone me at the office."

A PSYCHIATRIST RECOMMENDED THAT one of his patients, a depressed woman, take a vacation to get a change of scenery and lighten her mood. A week later, he received a postcard:

"Having a wonderful time. Why?"

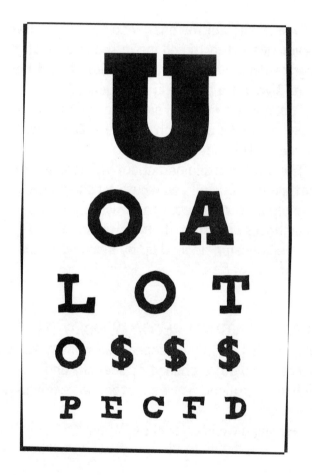

Doctor Goldstein and his wife were having dinner at an upscale restaurant when an attractive young blonde walked by, smiled at the doctor, and murmured, "Hi Sammy."

His wife, somewhat irritated, asked, "And who is that?"

"That's my mistress," Dr. Goldstein replied matter-of-factly.

"You have a mistress?" his wife cried. "How long has this been going on?"

"About five years now," Dr. Goldstein calmly replied.

His wife was now in tears. "Five years? *Five years?* I'm going to see a lawyer tomorrow about a divorce. You'll be ruined."

Dr. Goldstein put down his fork. "Now think about this for a moment. If we divorce, we each get half of what we have. You won't have that big house, won't get a new Beemer every year, and you certainly won't be shopping and playing bridge all day with your so-called friends."

Just then a cute redhead walked by. "Hi, Sammy."

"And just who is that one?" his wife snapped.

"That's Bill Grant's mistress," Dr. Goldstein replied.

His wife paused. "Doctor Grant has a mistress, too?"

"About twelve years now."

His wife picked up her fork and continued to eat. "Ours is a lot prettier."

PATIENT: NURSE, DURING MY OPERATION, I heard the surgeon use a four-letter word that upset me very much.

Nurse: What word was that?

Patient: "Oops!"

The patient shook his doctor's hand in gratitude and said, "Since we are the best of friends, I would not want to insult you by offering payment. But I would like for you to know that I had mentioned you in my will."

"That is very kind of you," said the doctor, a

bit choked up. Then he added, "May I see that prescription I just gave you? I'd like to make a little change . . ."

MR. LYONS WAS ADMITTED TO THE hospital for a routine procedure and was surprised to see how much he enjoyed himself. He spent his days patting the bottoms of the pretty nurses, offering to show them his scars, and asking quite a few out to dinner upon his release.

One nurse finally had all she could stand of Mr. Lyons's crude behavior. "A pervert like you should be living in a house of prostitution!"

Mr. Lyons just grinned at her. "Well, it *would* be cheaper than the hospital, but I can't get my insurance to pay for it!"

Patient: Please tell me, doctor, am I getting better?

Doctor: I think so. But to be sure, let me feel your wallet.

A MAN WAS WALKING ALONG THE STREET one afternoon, when he was robbed and brutally beaten. He lay on the street, unconscious and bleeding.

While he was lying there, a number of pedestrians walked along, oblivious to this man's plight. A police officer passed by, but he crossed to the other side of the street without trying to help. Even a Boy Scout troop walked past the scene, but all they could do was snicker and point.

Finally, a psychologist walked by, spotted the man and ran up to him. He bent down and cried, "My God! Whoever did this needs help!"

Five-year-old Becky answered the door when the census taker came by. She told the census taker that her daddy was a doctor and wasn't home because he was performing an appendectomy.

"My," said the census taker, "that sure is a big word for a little girl. Do you know what that means?"

"Sure!" Becky eagerly replied. "Fifteen hundred bucks, and that doesn't even include the anesthesiologist!"

PHARMACIST HANDING A PRESCRIPTION to a customer: "Take one of these every four hours, or as often as you can get the cap off."

A doctor was introduced to a young man at a cocktail party.
"I want to thank you, Dr. Brennan," said the young man, heartily shaking the doctor's hand. "I gained great benefit from your treatment."

Dr. Brennan looked at him blankly. "I'm sorry," he finally said, embarrassed, "but I didn't think you were a patient of mine."

"No, I'm not," the man replied cheerfully. "But my uncle was, and I'm his heir!"

DOCTOR: WE NEED TO GET THESE PEOPLE to a hospital!
   Nurse: What is it?

Doctor: It's a big building with a lot of doctors, but that's not important now!

After discovering her young daughter, Sally, playing doctor with Harry, the boy next door, the angry mother grabbed Harry by the ear and dragged him to his house to confront his mother.

"At this age, it's only natural for young boys and girls to explore their sexuality by playing doctor," the neighbor soothed.

"Sexuality, hell!" the irate parent yelled. "He was taking out her appendix!"

A PRETTY YOUNG LADY NAMED NANCY just broke off her engagement to a young doctor.

"Do you mean to tell me," exclaimed her friend, "that he actually asked you to return all the presents?"

"Not only that," replied Nancy, "but he also sent me a bill for house calls."

A doctor apologized for keeping an elderly woman waiting so long in his office.
"That's all right," she said demurely. "I just thought you'd like to treat my illness while it was in its early stages."

DR. HARTWICK, A CARDIOLOGIST, CAME up with a new operating procedure that would cut down the time of heart surgery and cause less trauma to the patient. He was paid $50,000 to present his findings, and was highly praised by his peers when he first presented the procedure at a convention in Washington D.C. After being asked to do a few more presentations, Dr. Hartwick soon realized that it would be more lucrative to do lectures on his findings than to continue as a surgeon, so he dropped his practice and began to do the lectures full-time. Soon he was bringing in lots of money, and was able to purchase his own limousine and hire a driver.

One day, after he'd been doing the lecture circuit for about six months, his driver, Mike, turned to him and said, "You know, this is completely unfair."

"What do you mean?" asked Dr. Hartwick.

"Well, you get paid $50,000 every time you do this lecture, and that's more than I get paid in a year," replied Mike. Dr. Hartwick explained that this was a very complicated procedure and he was the only person able to give this lecture. "That's not true," Mike protested. "I've seen you do your lecture so many times that I know it by heart."

"Well, if that's the case, I'll tell you what. You do this lecture and you can keep the $50,000 if you do it right."

"Okay. You're on," Mike replied.

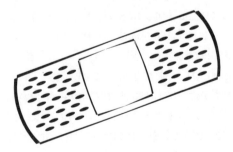

When they arrived at the lecture hall, Dr. Hartwick gave Mike his white coat, and Dr. Hartwick took Mike's hat and sat in the back of the room. Mike walked up to the podium, and nailed the presentation. Not only that, he also answered all the questions without missing a beat. Just when Mike thought he was done, an audience member, wearing a lab coat and tape-covered glasses, stood up and asked a complex question that the driver was unable to answer.

"You know," said Mike, "I have done this lecture 287 times and I have never been asked such a stupid question. As a matter of fact, that question is *so* stupid that I'm going to let my driver answer it."

While visiting a friend in the hospital, Cristina noticed several nurses all wearing pins designed to look like an apple. Curious, she asked one nurse what it signified.

"Nothing," she said with a smile. "It's just to keep the doctors away."